It's not impossible to go through a season unbeaten and I can't see why it's shocking to say that!
DOUBLE DOUBLE TO INVINCIBUBBLE
THE CONTINUED ADVENTURES OF A COOL CAT IN HIS MAGIC HAT

Published by
Legends Publishing

E-mail david@legendspublishing.net
Website www.legendspublishing.net

This book is dedicated to my friend Steve Chapman, who has been there for me consistently during some tough times.

Poorly Drawn Arsenal is a human being with questionable artistic skills and a love for Arsenal who combines the two into silly absurdity. He also finds writing about himself in third person to be weird. Anyway, he thanks Dave for the absurd opportunity to call himself a published illustrator. He has a weekly newsletter that wraps up the week for Arsenal at poorlydrawnarsenal.com.

FOREWORD

So a return to the tale of Arsene and his amazing magic hat,
To retread the legend of the Invincibles might seem foolish given that,
for two decades we have revelled in a season covered with glory,
And writers more accomplished than I have already told the story.

So I tip my hat to Arseblog and marvel at the talent of Amy,
But my telling of the 03/04 Premier League triumph will not be very samey,
I will not skimp on details, will cover every twist and turn that season took,
In a style more at home in a play of the Bard than in a footie book.

Every goal, in every match, our football so fluid and sublime,
The season introduced, and each month described in comedic rhyme,
And as a treat, to complement the couplets, I must have photos surely?
Hell no, far better to accompany my ode to The Invincibles, with Arsenal drawn poorly.

DAVE SEAGER

Prologue - Summer 2003

Arsene said it was possible to not lose once in a league season,
Most felt him mad, it had not been done in modern times for good reason,
Played 22, won 18, drawn four for Preston, dandy and fine,
But that was in the nineteenth century, the year 1889.

One hundred years later Arsenal won the league with the last kick of the game,
Could a club who loved the improbable make good on Wenger's claim?
2002/3 suggested perhaps not, as his team lost five matches,
Although his Gunners certainly enjoyed purple, unbeaten patches.

Let's put this one down to Double-winning fatigue,
Another FA Cup thanks to Bobby P, but runners up in the league,
An assumption then that the manager would freshen his talented squad,
A summer of activity expected, as anything less would be odd.

The legend that was Seaman was leaving, his heroic time was now done,
So big feet required to fill the shoes of the pony-tailed one,
2002 title-clinching hero Wiltord too was adding to our fears,
A new one-year deal being dangled but Sylvain wanted two years.

Was Wenger's policy for the over 30s now out of date?
Would he relax this summer before it was too late?
First order of business then to replace Big Dave,
No small task, given how much to our club he gave.

Expectations raised when Wenger swooped for Dortmund's Jens,
Lehmann, soon to be nicknamed Mad, with a reputation for saving pens,
A good start, but after finishing five points adrift of United, more business would be forthcoming,
Gooners had a wary eye on Old Trafford, whilst hoping for more incoming.

Anxieties amplified as Fergie made signing after signing,
Surely Wenger recognised his summer work could be season defining,
United added Saha, Howard and secured Kleberson, a World Cup winner,
By comparison Arsenal's squad was looking somewhat thinner.

They added some talented kid called Ronaldo, and you may also remember,
A Cameroonian so bad they named him twice, Eric Djemba Djemba!
The exit door at Highbury was active with senior pros departing,
With no one coming the other way, when were the signings starting?

Crazy Horse Luzhnyi went to Wolves, he never let us down,
Igor sent out for a Belgian loan, no tears to lose that clown,
Defensively, Arsene was leaving us light, with Gio perhaps off to Camp Nou,
Van B was our left-back cover for Cole, but surely, we needed two.

An injury away from Cygan being called upon every week, with Keown getting older,
Two new 18-year-olds Arsene? Clichy and Senderos, surely too much responsibility for them to shoulder,
What card was hidden up Arsene's sleeve to ensure we were in the title race?
Another Lauren style positional masterstroke, Kolo Toure was Wenger's ace.

In the last three pre-season warm up matches, the Kolo and Sol partnership grew,
We worried no longer as it soon became obvious that once again - Arsene knew!
The truth, Le Prof had earned our trust, and it paid to remember that,
Whilst Fergie had the money and a big red nose, Le Prof had a Magic Hat!

Important author's note:
What follows is an accurate, goal-by-goal romp through Arsenal's 2003/4
38-match Premier League campaign only. Other competitions will be largely ignored.

A Not So Friendly Community Shield

10th August, Cardiff, Millennium Stadium.

No match between these two giants was ever a friendly affair,
No trophy required to ensure the players would care,
Wenger and Fergie, friends now, but arch enemies then,
Yellow cards or red, not a case of if, more of when?

Inside a minute was the answer, Phil Neville the pantomime baddie,
No one shouted 'behind you' as he crunched into Paddy,
Only two minutes in, Solskjaer suffered a similar fate,
It would be kind to Ashley Cole to say he was late.

Ref Steve Bennett had to be on top of his game,
United v Arsenal back then was always the same,
Later on, forgotten man Franny Jeffers, saw red,
His mortally wounded Highbury career, at that moment dead.

Along with the physicality though, we witnessed the flair,
With both teams' title credentials quite obviously there,
A corner flicked on by Keane allowed Silvestre to score with his head,
Our new centre back Toure lost his man, it had to be said.

Minutes later Vieira fouled by Butt, some 30 yards out,
Out of range for mere mortals, but with Thierry, a shout,
Debutant Howard placed his wall carefully, it helped not a jot,
as Henry arrowed the ball into the corner, an unsavable shot.

A feisty feast after 90 minutes saw the teams undivided,
The destination of the Shield by penalties would be decided,
Van Nistlerooy failed from the spot, unheard of back then,
Sadly, Howard saved from Gio and then up against Bobby he did it again.

The curtain-raiser completed, let the real season begin,
United were the favourites, but the difference between the teams, paper thin,
Still doubts over our squad depth, but keep the faith we must,
After the beautiful football and glory, he brought us, in Arsene we must trust!

August

16th August Everton (H)

An expectant Highbury faithful waited, 38,000 packed in,
A home start in the North London sun, all hoping for that win,
Bergkamp had started in Cardiff, so we all assumed the same,
Surprised therefore to see Henry alongside contract rebel Sylvain.

Wiltord, our Old Trafford hero, we are forever in his debt,
Though that he kicked off this campaign, many fans forget.
The Gunners marauding in attack, the start was super bright,
Wenger's Arsenal in full flow, a quite magnificent sight.

Then after 25 the task made harder, Gravesen through on goal,
Unceremoniously hauled down by Arsenal's last man, Super Sol.
Pressure relieved before half-time, and not saying it was planned!
Henry's skill in the box, flicked the ball right onto Stubbs' hand.

Thierry stepped up to ease the doubts, so often saviour in red and white,
He sent their keeper the wrong way, ex-Gooner, Richard Wright,

Everton battled bravely, we needed another for sure,
We all remembered what Rooney had done to us the very year before.

The Everton super-kid, on after the break to add to their attack,
Wiltord sacrificed for Keown to steady us at the back,
Pires calmed the nerves, and the crowd once again were rocking,
Bobby so cool under pressure after some heroic Everton blocking.

A late Radzinski effort left us praying for the final whistle,
A harder opener than it should have been due to another dismissal,
The media in a frenzy over the 51st red card of Arsene's reign,
Ignored by Gooners laughing that we won with ten again!

24th August Middlesbrough (A)

This trip to the North-East ended up quite a romp,
Boro blown away by a rampant Arsenal in all their pomp,
Over as a contest within 22 majestic minutes of play,
Three early goals left us hoping for a hatful that day.

Fast starting to get the job done in double-quick time,
Before easing of the throttle was this team at their prime,

A tap in for Henry after Schwarzer denied our Freddie,
Only five minutes on the clock, poor Boro, just were not ready,
Then Cole and Pires combined superbly on the left, so often the case,
The latter lofting his cross over five forlorn defenders for Gilberto's volley of precision and pace.

The third was vintage Gunners, and made solely en France,
Bobby and Thierry presenting Sylvain his chance,
And whilst his compatriots role in the build-up I would never diminish,
A special mentioned reserved for Wiltord's deftly angled cushioned finish.

The home side fought well but seldom threatened to score,
The traveling fans desperate for at least one or two more,
They got want they hoped for, Ljungberg unselfishly squared from the right,
Leaving that man again, Wiltord, to put the match out of sight.

The diminutive striker desperate to show Wenger he deserved two more years,
Bergkamp kept firmly on the bench, while Sylvain went through the gears,
The Ice Man having to make do with a cameo when the match was already won,
We all pondered how long this would be the case, but it didn't spoil our fun.

27th August Aston Villa (H)

Next up the Villans, managed by our own legend O'Leary
Only three days' rest for the team, would they be weary?
A flying Gunners start suggested not,
An early save from Sorensen from Henry's shot.

The constant attacking continued unabashed,
On 15, Freddie's super lob off the cross bar crashed,
But Villa defended stoutly and kept us at bay,
Goalless at half-time was this not to be our day?

O2

Quite often this team's goals were things of beauty, it has to be said,
On this day, the breakthrough was a corner from Pires onto Sol's head,
The visitors battled bravely and still carried a threat,
Pablo Angel was lively, but we had no need to fret.

Wenger knew it was time and he made the decision,
On 67 minutes he sent for Dennis, we needed his vision,
And in injury time the Ice Man set up his partner Henry,
The points wrapped up at the death, three wins from three.

31st August Man City (A)

It looked tough on paper, and it proved to be so,
Former Gunner Anelka was certainly keen to put on a show,
Keegan's men started swiftly, Wenger's team more slowly,
Pressure paid off when Lauren scored passed his own goalie.

No blame for Jens who had already impressed the fans,
Tough following Seaman, but we felt in safe hands,
Losing such a servant as Big Dave was of course a pity,
But no mercy that day as he was in goal for Man City,

We didn't create a chance until the 40-minute mark,
An uncharacteristic Henry miss, even the King had no spark,
The second period was an altogether different affair,
No doubt Le Prof's halftime chat gave his players a scare.

Cole nicked the ball off Distin to set up Wiltord,
One Sylvain robbed and the other one scored,
The winner duly arrived, thanks to our Super Swede,
Sadly, an unconvincing Seaman saw his new team concede.

He dived at the feet of Pires and missed the ball completely,
Which allowed our Freddie to finish it neatly,
He was booked for celebrating with the away fans, he is still everywhere,
We still loved our Freddie, even without his red hair!

One month gone, four played and four won,
So far so good Arsene and we're having so much fun!

P4 - WWWW

September

13th September Portsmouth (H)

Back after a break and on paper an easier team to play,
Pompey back in the big time after 15 years away,
The boss maybe thought so as he brought in three fresh faces,
No Gilberto, Wiltord or Freddie, with Edu, Bergkamp and Parlour in their places.

But Redknapp's Portsmouth were also unbeaten and made the better start,
The early running was made by them, giving the visiting fans good heart,
We assumed they would come to Highbury and park the proverbial bus,
Sick to our stomachs when Sheringham scored and celebrated in front of us.

They were giving Toure and Campbell a torrid time, truth be told,
We had expected respectful and timid, but they arrived confident and bold.

It took a bit of fortune for Arsenal to stop the rot
Henry gratefully equalising from the penalty spot
A clumsy tackle from Stefanovic on Pires, he never got the ball,
To be honest, the contact was minimal to cause such a theatrical fall!

Thierry beat Hislop once but just to add some spice,
The ref saw a player encroaching, so he had to do so twice.
Honours even at the break, but after Arsenal went up a gear or two,
Hislop saving twice from Dennis, from Thierry and a free kick from Edu.

The team pressed hard for the winner, but on this day, it was not to be,
One point kept the Gunners top, but they would have hoped for three,
Ultimately controversial and Pompey may have labelled our Bobby a cheat,
How valuable then would it be, that our French winger could not stay on his feet?

21st September Man United (A)

In autumn 1990 Arsenal had a battle at Old Trafford and went on to glory,
Now though the two teams were both title contenders, an entirely different story,
23 years earlier Graham's team were docked points for their part,
Recent matches had been equally fierce, we were not anticipating Arsene's art.

Fergie and Wenger's teams, giants at war, trading blow for blow,
The nation would be watching, two juggernauts on show,
With no Campbell for personal reasons, Wenger went for experience and grit,
Bergkamp in with battle-hardened Parlour and Keown ready to do their bit.

10

Obvious from the first minute there was no place for faint of heart,
Both sets of players committed and tackling hard right from the start,
United skipper Keane was the first player to be booked, and wouldn't be the last,
Crunching challenges left and right, the match both physical and fast.

In fairness, the home side looked the more likely, but bravo Arsenal's defence,
Giggs and van Nistlerooy went close but veteran hero Keown was simply immense,
A frustrated Dutch striker squared up with Lehmann, he was not a happy fellow,
At this stage, it was only handbags, but both earned themselves a yellow.

In the last 15 minutes crazy referring should have handed victory to United,
But a sense of gross injustice saw a fire in the Arsenal players ignited,
Vieira booked for a foul on Fortune with 13 minutes left to play,
Paddy was then jumped on by van Nistlerooy, much to our captain's dismay.

Our skipper flicked an angry leg as he hit the ground so hard,
Sadly, it gave referee Bennett an excuse to pull out the second yellow card,
It was so obvious the Dutch striker had made no attempt to play the ball,
The Arsenal players incensed, and what followed was an unsightly brawl.

A feeling of being wronged weighed on the team but the spirt was undiminished,
Ten minutes plus to hold out one man down, the drama far from finished,
In injury time, the softest of pens, Keown adjudged to have tugged Forlan's shirt,
No time for the Gunners to respond if our 'favourite Dutchman' could convert.

Was it down to Mad Jens to ensure this angry affair did not end with a loss?
To preserve the belief in an unbeaten season, predicted by his new boss,
He gave Ruud the eyes, moved left and right to unnerve the United star,
It must have worked as Jens watched the penalty crashing off the bar.

Oh, the scenes as Keown roared in the distraught striker's face,
And the fracas that followed the final whistle were probably a disgrace,
But we fans loved Martin Keown, so often our saviour,
Of course, we forgave him and his peers the unsightly behaviour.

The truth is the togetherness further forged in the Old Trafford affray,
Would hold this amazing team in good stead for many a day,
Both managers and players felt justified to moan,
After 'The Battle of Old Trafford', as it soon became known.

Wenger suggested Van the Man had feigned contact to get Paddy his red,
In response, the Dutch striker's innocence Ferguson pled,
The FA threw the book at the Arsenal and six players for improper conduct,
Would this be 1990 again with them deciding it was points to deduct?

Instead, a £175k hit for Arsenal, the largest club fine ever imposed,
Alongside, hefty fines and suspensions for our naughty players were proposed,
Lauren suffered the most, charged with violent behaviour not once, but twice,
His actions resulting in a fine and future four-match ban, a heavy price.

Martin Keown also hit in the pocket, and three matches to be missed,
The FA Board anxious that Arsenal's ill-discipline would not persist,
Vieira and the Romford Pele also fined with one-match bans,
Surely all the players missing would impact Arsene's plans.

Cole escaped a suspension and the charges against Mad Jens were dropped,
However, despite all this, the Premier League table Arsenal still topped!

26th September Newcastle United (H)

With Newcastle the visitors, Arsenal's behaviour was under the microscope,
The media suggesting our ill-discipline would dent our Premier League hope,
In anticipation of a poor reaction, the whole football world was looking,
So, Arsene's boys gave them a win without one single booking!

As a point of reference, all six players charged earlier in the week,
Trusted to continue the team's unbeaten streak,
On 18, Henry opened the scoring after a mistake from Titus Bramble,
Newcastle level through Robert, after a goal-mouth scramble.

Arsenal suffered a serious blow when Paddy limped off holding his thigh,
Time to see how the Gunners would cope without their main guy,
So difficult to watch the best midfielder in Europe depart,
Having the quality of Edu to join Gilberto, though, did give us heart.

So nearly back ahead, when of O'Brien's slip, Freddie made the most,
Only to see his stunning curled chip come back off the post,
Midway through the second half Arsenal once again led,
A perfect Pires free kick found Gilberto Silva's head.

Amazing his first goal for the club in front of his home crowd,
In recognition of the fact, the fan's response was loud,
We only had four minutes in the popular Brazilian's success to revel,
When a screamer from Bernard brought the Magpies level.

With ten remaining on the clock, the visitors handed the game to us when,
The hapless Jenas handled from a corner, an obvious pen.

I could say Henry beating their keeper was a Given,
Perhaps for this Shay awful pun, I can be forgiven,
Two months of the season passed and seven matches, no loss,
Too early to be dreaming about the prediction of Le Boss?

P7- WWWWDDW

October

4th October Liverpool (A)

We began the month one point clear at the top of the Premier League,
Liverpool were not the team they used to be but still not an easy trip,
Bergkamp was unavailable and Wenger surprised us with double French,
Henry and young Aliadiere, leaving Wiltord on the bench.

A daunting day for the youngster, trusted to prove his worth,
Pires in for Ljungberg, with Parlour keeping his starting berth,
Sol returned to re-join Kolo with the redoubtable Keown missing out,
Would the reshuffle affect the Gunners and give the Reds a shout?

The early running was made by the home team for sure,
Harry Kewell executing a perfect volley past Lehmann to score,
Liverpool bossed the first half hour and should have gone further ahead,
Some good saves from Jens, but mostly poor finishing, it has to be said.

But after 30 minutes, much to the Anfield Reds frustration,
They learned the harsh lesson that you must score in periods of domination,

A Pires free kick deflected off Edu and took a swerve,
Onto Hypia's head and into the goal, an equaliser we did not deserve.

Second-half injuries to Smicer and Owen saw Liverpool come unstuck,
In a long season, even the best teams need the occasional bit of luck,
Though you also get rewarded for hard work, skill, and endeavour,
There was no good fortune involved in Arsenal's winner, whatsoever.

Player of the Year 2002, by his peers, duly elected,
We all knew Pires capable of the most unexpected,
But his curling, out to in, strike past a flailing Dudek, let's be perfectly clear,
Quite simply one of the finest goals of 2003 or any year.

An important win away that afternoon, and it is always stressed,
The truly great teams find a way to win when not at their best.

18th October Chelsea (H)

Next up the noisy noveau-riche neighbours from Sloane Square,
Saved, then bank rolled, by an oily Russian billionaire,

Chelsea, pushing hard to join the established elite,
Like Wenger's Arsenal, yet to taste Premier League defeat.

Ludicrous amounts of money to spend, many felt it obscene
Precocious parvenues or serious contenders, it remained to be seen.
With Paddy still suspended, Parlour proudly wore the armband in his stead,
But it was Vieira's midfield replacement, Edu who was to put Arsenal ahead,

The Gunners started so well, fast out of the blocks,
Then a handball by Glen Johnson just outside the box.
Not a Brazilian wonder free kick, but the power on the shot was enough,
To deflect the ball past Cudicini off the foot of a forlorn Damien Duff,

To be fair to the visitors, their response was swift and emphatic,
A power driver from Hernan Crespo left Jens Lehmann quite static.
The remainder of the first half saw two teams slugging it out blow for blow,
For the neutral, the league's top sides putting on quite a show.

Our boys stepped it up after half time, tightening their grip on the day,
But we saw enough to know that our West London rivals were in the race to stay,

O2

The Boss acknowledged the adversary with attacking subs on 66,
A real signal of intent with three strikers then in the mix.

Parlour and Wiltord off and Bergkamp and Kanu on to win the match,
Could these two wily old campaigners this tough opponent dispatch?
Yes, was the answer, their impact was decisive and swift,
A super through ball from Kanu and Edu presented Henry a gift.

We were still wondering how Cudicini had saved Thierry's shot,
Thankfully, while we were scratching our heads, Bergkamp was not,
The quick-thinking Dutch maestro's free kick sent Pires away on the wing,
His crossed fumbled by the Italian Keeper at the feet of the King.

Cudicini, in a minute from hero to cardinal sinner,
His absolute howler had handed the home team their valuable winner,
So the Arsenal held their nerve, were victors that day and deserved,
Yet, one could not help but feel that Chelsea's notice of intent had been served.

October 26th Charlton Athletic (A)

A Sunday afternoon stroll on paper proved not to be such a breeze,
In fact, the well-drilled Addicks had won their previous three with ease,

Curbishley had blended an industrious ethos and added Di Canio flair,
The talismanic Italian put the hosts one up, with a nonchalant air.

Lauren adjudged to have tripped Matt Holland; a penalty awarded,
A Panenka past Jens saw Charlton's early enterprise rewarded,
With the Henry and Bergkamp partnership again restored,
Arsenal bounced back with some urgency, and it was the Frenchman who scored.

To coin a phrase, he had the Charlton defence on toast,
Before he unleashed a screamer which thudded back off the post,
In all honesty we were used to having so much brilliance to admire,
For seasons now, our balletic Number 14 had been on fire.

To describe his free kick as 'a worldie' would not be speaking too highly,
Curled into 'top bins' away from the despairing fingers of Dean Kiely,
The second half was hard fought, and in other circumstances,
Either team might have snatched the win, if they had converted chances.

Our twinkled-toed substitute Kanu might have won it at the death
Clean through, only to shoot tamely at the keeper as the Valley held its breath

A point was enough to regain top spot and another London derby without a loss
Since 2002, 22 London matches without being beaten, truly the Capital's boss

As October drew to a close, perhaps some clairvoyancy news
Arsenal were the only team of the 92 in the English leagues so far, not to lose

P10- WWWWDDWWWD

November

November 1st Leeds United (A)

The Arsenal team set off for Yorkshire, the collective mind set on revenge,
The home defeat by Leeds in May was a bitter one to avenge,
Yes, we had lifted the FA Cup soon after, but still our season blighted,
We had been neck and neck in the title race until that loss handed it to United.

For Wenger, football was indeed art, but he offered no hard directive,
Yes, he preferred it beautiful, but he also loved it effective,
So a long ball from Cole, and the pace of Henry, saw him in the clear,
A miss was a rarity one-on-one for the 2003 PFA Player of the Year.

Route One it may have been, but the away fans were not complaining,
One down after only eight minutes, the effect on the Leeds team was draining,
Less than ten later, winning the ball in our own area, we were two ahead,
No one breaks quite like Arsenal, Martin Tyler in commentary said.

Bergkamp, down the line to Ljungberg, forward he was driving,
One moment he was on his own, an instant later, he had three arriving,
His ball bypassed Silva and Henry, no matter as Bobby was waiting there,
A lovely shot back across the goal saw a Robinson dive of despair.

Leeds toiled manfully trying to respond but there really was no way back,
Every time they lost the ball, the Gunners sprang from defence to attack,
Another fast break for number three saw Dennis hit the upright,
The ball ricocheted to Thierry, for the defenders a depressing sight.

The finish from the best striker in the land was clinical and swift,
No one at Elland Road believed for a second that he would not accept the gift,
Before half time Henry might have sealed a hat-trick but shot over the bar,
Perhaps he could miss occasionally, our majestic, dazzling star.

Peter Reid half-time team talk had an effect, the home side showed more intent,
But it was all meaningless with Arsenal in this mood, and that was how it went,
Despite Leeds' early effort, it was not a case of if we would score but when,
Five minutes of the home team's bluster before Arsenal fired home again.

A Bergkamp freekick from the right, which Pires cut back, such vision!
His deflected pass found Gilberto, who from close range, finished with precision,
A consolation from Alan Smith which the Leeds fans who had stayed greeted,
Arsenal missed more chances if truth be told but the revenge mission was completed.

Top of the league by a point, and a huge match next at Highbury
The visitors being Spurs, for that fixture it would never be 'The Library'.

November 8th Tottenham (H)

The noisy neighbours from Middlesex swaggered (well, more staggered) into town,
Believing (well more like hoping) that they could take us down,
We all knew though that form in this match might not be in the equation,
Spurs had not won at our place in 11 visits, could the 12th be the occasion?

Wenger selection surprised us, Bergkamp out, with Kanu coming in,
One great man for another, surely Spurs chances would be thin?
Still without captain Paddy, veteran Parlour preferred to Edu,
Nervous ahead of kick off, but telling ourselves, Arsene knew!

To be fair to Spurs they were fast out of the blocks, and in four minutes led,
Sick Note Anderton scored from close range, back from his hospital bed,
Hate to admit it but they had us rattled, our defence was poor, even Sol,
Thank goodness their summer signing Postiga was so woeful in front of goal.

Misplaced back passes from Lauren twice put the Portuguese striker through,
£6.5 million on a centre forward with the predatory nature of a shrew,
Tempers frayed, nothing new of course, this fixture always raised the blood,
Theatrical Pires, Carr's arm on Henry's throat and many a tackle with high stud.

Keller saved once from Henry, but a rare first half with Arsenal second best,
But up to Le Prof, no doubt his unflustered talk, would see the situation addressed,
No instant up-turn evident, amazingly the visitors had the edge,
Until on 69 up stepped the Romford Pele, his boot like a chipping wedge.

Parlour's lofted pass and a perfectly timed run saw Henry clear,
Keller saved from the Thierry but guess who was lurking near,
He always scores against the Spuds, no need for us to fret,
Bobby P on hand to smash the ball into the roof of the net.

Dennis on for Gilberto then, Arsenal now three strong in attack,
Not our best on the pitch that day, but in courage we would never lack,

The clock ticked on, frustration grew, would honours end up even?
No was the answer, thanks to a hapless Irish chap by the name of Stephen,
For the equaliser it was Carr who failed to move up, playing Henry onside,
For the winner it was poor Stephen again, and our joy we could not hide.

A sweeping move saw Kanu find Freddie on the left, 25 yards out,
Remembering Wembley 2002, what came next was never in doubt,
He cut inside, unleashed a goal-bound drive, no less than we expected
Which hit Stephen's outstretched leg, and over Keller deflected

The Old Enemy had pushed us hard to be fair and forced us to dig deep,
One set of fans partied hard into the night, the other into their beers did weep,
You need some luck to win the league and we had our share that day,
Is that like my team making me happy, even when the skies are grey?

November 22nd Birmingham City (A)

It was the day that the Old Trafford suspensions began,
It meant a debut for young Clichy and a start for Cygan,
A debutant left back, playing in midfield with Edu, far from ideal,
Was our concern at the lack of summer signings about to get real?

Arsene's 400th match as Gunners' boss, an occasion to be noted,
That the task was tougher with players missing could not be sugar-coated,
The Blues flying high under Bruce were playing for more than pride,
At start of play, 5th in the table, a test for Arsenal's much-changed side.

Thank Goodness for Freddie, settling our nerves with such class,
A perfect start on four minutes from Henry's perfectly weighted pass,
A previously raucous St Andrews was now stunned and subdued,
A depleted Arsenal's calmness and assurance, the early goal had renewed.

The hosts had only conceded 8 in 12 in the league until then,
Only their keeper saving brilliantly from Henry stopped 9 becoming 10,
With a good defensive record, twas in attack that Birmingham were toothless,
But then again, they had not played The Arsenal, and we could be ruthless.

The home team held out at 0-1, until a welcome half-time whistle blew,
Arsenal returned invigorated and began turning the screw,
Only more saves from keeper Maik Taylor and some desperate defending,
Prevented an increasingly confident Arsenal, their lead from extending.

Then after 80 minutes, the majesty of Bergkamp, skipper on the day,
A quick break started by substitute Kanu, that saw Henry send Dennis on his way,
The Ice Man had to run from the halfway line, away from a chasing pack,
Before a delightfully dinked finish left Birmingham with no way back.

With minutes to go, Pires finished the job by adding a third
Three Arsenal goals, yet none for our Number 14, seemed so absurd,
But then I neglected to mention that it was he that set up Bobby P,
So, whilst not actually scoring himself that day, he assisted all three!

30th November Fulham (H)

Still leading the pack but only a point ahead of the West London Blues,
With another London Derby against West London's other big news,
Fulham had sacked Tigana, the football under him had been grim,
Threw Chris Coleman in the management deep end and found that he could swim.

Cole was back on the left and Pascal Cygan retained his place,
Gilberto returned to partner Edu, a midfield of Brazilian grace,
Optimism was high at Highbury, our front four all were flying,
Henry, Bergkamp, Ljungberg, and Pires would take some denying.

But denied we were again and again not by profligacy, post, or bar,
No, by an incredible Dutch giant by the name of Van der Sar,
It was not for lack of attacking intent we didn't get the goal we craved,
Fulham's magnificent shot-stopper equal to all, 12 efforts on target saved.

Wenger threw the kitchen sink at Fulham late on, four strikers were on show,
Aliadiere and Kanu joining Thierry and Dennis, the last two dice to throw,
Sometimes you just have to tip your hat to a magnificent display,
Even Wenger's magic hat was tipped to Edwin that November day.

To truly grasp the magnitude of Arsenal's failure to score,
Under Arsene they had scored in 46 successive home fixtures before,
Still unbeaten, but frustrated, an annoying two home points to drop,
And that draw, after three great wins, saw Chelsea end November top.

P14 - WWWWDDWWWDWWWD

December

6th December Leicester (A)

Still unbeaten as we entered month five of the Premier League campaign,
Yet surprisingly not top, those oil-backed neighbours a genuine pain,
Would December be the month to sort out the men from the boys,
We knew we were the real deal, but were Chelsea simply annoying noise?

No Vieira or Henry for our visit to mid-table Leicester,
With Toure still at right back, Sol continued with Uncle Fester,
We needed true depth and not every player in the squad could be a superstar,
To be fair to Pascal Cygan he had been letting no one down thus far.

Perhaps a surprise though, as Keown was again available at the back,
But more of a shock to see Aliadiere get the nod to partner Dennis in attack,
The new Walkers stadium record broken, over 32 thousand came that day,
They only came to see the Arsenal was all we needed to say.

An uncomfortable start with our makeshift defence raising a first-half sweat,
Scowcroft and veteran Sir Les of the Ferdinand, a dual aerial threat,
In fairness they harried and chased, refusing to let us play,
It was a stalemate at the break, but the Foxes had held sway.

We needed to raise our game; surely, we would improve after the break,
Then soon after the restart, had Big Sol made a costly mistake?
When Marcus Bent tumbled in the box, we knew what was coming next,
But Leicester appeals fell on deaf ears, the ref forgot his specs!

Reprieved and relieved, the Gunners aimed to take advantage of their luck,
Ten minutes later and to Leicester's dismay, the Arsenal struck,
Bergkamp's skills on the left led their defenders a merry dance,
The vision to see Gilberto's run, the Brazilian's header gave Walker no chance,

Our first chance brought a goal and confidence quickly grew.
The same Dutch and Brazilian pair so nearly made it two,
A freekick from Dennis, a scissor-kick from Silva, what a save by Walker,
The Foxes keeper denying a thing of beauty, it would have been a corker.

The home team had to chase the game, which left us spaces to exploit,
Something at which this Arsenal team was usually so adroit,
Wiltord back and on for young Jeremie, a clear show of attacking intent,
But only five minutes later, Cole scythed down Thatcher, we all knew what it meant,

If any team knew how to hold out a player down, it was Arsene Wenger's men,
But one day our luck would run out, and we would not hold out with ten,
That December afternoon at the Walker's stadium proved to be that day,
A 90th minute ball flicked on for Craig Hignett saw the Foxes have the final say.

With key players out or playing out of position, and the squad players on show,
Was this outcome two points lost, or one point gained, at this stage, hard to know.

December 14th Blackburn (H)

The team without their main man had certainly kept their nerve,
The blessing of having the quality of Edu as a first reserve,
But when all is said and done, there really was only one midfield daddy,
So, it was with huge joy, after eight matches without him, we welcomed back Paddy.

Still no Ralph Lauren, so Kolo stayed on the right, and Pascal is Wenger's guy,
Fester keeping a warrior on the bench, veteran Keown probably wondered why,
Dennis and Thierry back in tandem, hoping to put Rovers to the sword,
Henry that week nominated for the World Player of the Year award.

Yet the visitors started oh so well, an old enemy to the fore,
Only Dwight Yorke will know, after 20 seconds, how he failed to score,
Their early pressure came to nowt, and soon poor Souness would be fuming,
The early storm was weathered, and normal service would be resuming.

He knew against this Arsenal team, you had to score during your purple patches,
At Highbury (or anywhere actually) this team were not losing matches,
Our first attack saw our stand-in full back Toure rampaging down the right
The Ivorian's athletic power at full tilt, a rare and beautiful sight

Into the area he strode, cutting back to Dennis who had found space,
Instant control gave the Ice Man time to slide home with his customary grace,
Then a searching cross from Freddie was only partially headed clear,
Just as far Pires on the edge of the area, a sight any defence would fear.

TOURE
28

Bobby unleashed a rasping, curling drive, Friedel could only watch its flight,
The American shot-stopper much relieved to see it crash back off the upright,
The Rovers keeper was immense that day, a Rovers hero in their time of need,
Save upon save, then a block from Henry, preventing Arsenal doubling their lead.

It continued the same after the break, red and white attacking waves persisting,
Our nemesis Friedel denying Ljungberg, the brilliant Bergkamp as ever assisting,
It was one-way Arsenal traffic, but the Blackburn parked bus remained strong,
A further breakthrough must come we thought, but that day we were wrong.

In fact, the Rovers soaked up all our efforts, then hit us smartly on the break,
Thank goodness Mad Jens stayed alert, so long without a save to make,
A full stretch dive on 70 minutes, his fingertips kept Barry Ferguson's shot out,
That he was the right man to replace Big Dave, was truly no longer in doubt.

Then a reaction block from Craig Short's header, Lehmann, what a star!
We all watched with great relief, as Yorke scooped the parried ball over the bar,
It was not the easy Sunday stroll in the park expected, too much extra stress,
But though it was far from vintage Arsenal, it was three points nonetheless.

Fergie's boys had gone top the day before, a three-horse race ignited,
So our hard-fought victory saw us back at the summit, leapfrogging Chelsea and United.

20th December Bolton (A)

There was undoubtedly some rancour and recent history between the teams,
It would be fair to say Big Sam and Le Prof ran quite different regimes,
Arsene felt that football should be a thing of beauty akin to creating art,
With Allardyce it was more painting by numbers but with no less heart.

His team though had proved to have Arsenal's number and got under our skin,
April's draw at the Reebok had pretty much put our title challenge in the bin,
The defence was still looking frail with Cole injured and Lauren not quite fit,
A back line of Clichy joining Sol, Pascal and Kolo looked inexperienced we had to admit.

Particularly facing old timers with class like Campo, Okocha, Djorkaeff and co,
Add in Kevin Davies, there was not a trick in the book these lot did not know,
It would be fair to say that Arsenal were not at the races and well below par,
Lehmann kept us in it, and when beaten by Djorkaeff, we were saved by the bar.

No threat from the Gunners, with a first-choice midfield and attack on show,
As the first half drew to a close, we all wanted the whistle to blow,
But then in the 45th minute a devastating break gave us back a little pride,
Vieira striding out, fed Henry, who crossed for Freddie to head narrowly wide.

The flurry at the end of the first period and Wenger's chat did the trick,
Heads were up, the tempo was better, and the passing was quick,
A last-ditch tackle by Simon Charlton prevented Henry opening the scoring,
At last, our midfield imposing themselves, the fans hope was restoring.

Bergkamp stole possession, his vision found Henry racing down the right wing,
From defence to attack in seconds, who could catch up with the King?
The answer was the Super Swede arriving to receive a squared pass,
Jaaskelainen saved from Freddie, their shot stopper had always been class.

Sadly, for the heroic Fin, he could only watch, whilst helpless on the floor,
As his save rebounded straight to Pires, who pounced quickly to score,
The home team roared on by the Reebok faithful would not lie down and die,
One look at Big Sam chewing a wasp in the dugout will probably tell you why.

His team played to the end and in fairness they likely deserved their reward,
He brought on an extra striker, Henrick Pederson who put us to the sword,
A screamer of a volley from the Dane, as sweetly struck as any you will see,
Meant that Arsenal, still unbeaten, returned to London with one point, not three.

26th December Wolves (H)

Time to renew the title challenge, the boys, ready, willing, and able,
The busy pre-Christmas programme had seen Man United back atop the table,
The frenetic festive programme showed no let up with two matches in four days,
First up were rock-bottom Wolves, so surely back to winning ways.

The Boxing Day match is always special, the home fans out in full force,
Delighted to offer a Highbury welcome to Luzhny, the Crazy Horse,
Henry grabbed the headlines but how good was Vieira, seriously?
One word for how Paddy dominated this match and that would be imperiously.

Thierry had an effort tipped over the bar as early as minute four,
The Wolves defence at sixes and sevens, the whole team in fact was poor,
The pressure paid off after 13 minutes, it had only been a matter of time,
A Craddock OG, after a shot from Paddy, gave Wolves a mountain to climb.

Then our skipper robbed the hapless Craddock and strode toward the box,
Leaving gold shirts trailing in his wake, he calmly set up Henry, our fox,
We all hoped for goals galore to continue the Christmas celebration,
For the visitors, the second half was all about damage limitation.

!
OH NO
O2

Ten Wolves players behind the ball had Arsenal huffing and puffing,
Thoughts then drifting to home for sandwiches filled with turkey and stuffing,
But of course one man that afternoon would not let the performance drift,
Paddy broke up play, as he had all day, to offer hope of a parting Christmas gift.

He passed on to Edu, who found Henry, the French genius still had so much to do,
He turned the defenders inside and out, and what came next, we all knew,
The passed shot from the left into the right-hand corner of the net,
It was Thierry's 12th in the league, and not at halfway yet.

29th December Southampton (A)

The starting 11 was unchanged for the final match of the year,
Though to hear Lauren announced on the bench caused a huge cheer,
Toure had deputised well for our popular first choice from Cameroon,
And to see him in the squad suggested he would be ready soon.

Gilberto was still out with a knock, so Parlour deputised once more
Preferred over Edu to partner Paddy, we had such a strong midfield four,
The Saints had lost out in the FA Cup in May but were going well in the league,
Though ahead of the match, Strachan was bemoaning injuries and squad fatigue.

His long leg nicked the ball ahead of Unsworth's lunge, he made it look a stroll,
Steering his first of the league campaign past a diving Martyn in the Everton goal,
Kanu may not have been a starter that often but he never once complained,
And it is with squad contributors like him that title challenges are sustained.

Everton at home were far from defensive and showed attacking flair,
With the giant Big Dunc, Radzinski, and Rooney, the counter was always there,
Henry's pace bothered the Toffees, but to be fair Rooney was an equal threat,
More than once the young man went close, the home team in Lehmann's debt.

A day where Thierry was the creator and sadly his colleagues could not convert,
The longer it went without the second goal, you feared we might get hurt,
Moyes must have sensed it, adding Arsenal loanee Jeffers to the fray,
With 4 strikers on the pitch, he hoped to make Arsenal's profligacy pay.

Everton's courage at Highbury had to be begrudgingly admired,
And they got their rewarded on 75, with the Arsenal backline seeming tired,
Route one to Big Dunc, headed on to Jeffers to shoot, as Ashley sadly slipped,
Jens saved, but Radzinski pounced on the rebound, an equaliser not in our script.

A return for Gilberto and Edu also on, as Wenger tried to reshuffle for the win,
Not our day and perhaps two points dropped, but you have to take it on the chin,
Three points behind the leaders United, but the unbeaten run got longer,
With only a three-day turnaround this time, we needed to come back stronger.

O2
25

18th January Aston Villa (A)

Still no Dennis, so recent positive impacts saw Kanu selected,
The opposition with Pablo Angel in form had to be respected,
Kolo not quite fit enough to start, that news no longer such a blow,
With the season's pleasant surprise Cygan, starting his tenth league match in a row.

The hosts began brightly with Gareth Barry impressing in the midfield tussle,
But as the first half progressed Vieira and Co began to flex their greater muscle,
First a sensational tip over from Sorensen was in in itself the only reason,
Why a rasping volley from Pires was not a contender for goal of the season.

Then a dangerous tackle on Paddy gave Arsenal a free kick on the edge of the D,
Undoubtedly, it was well within the range of a certain Thierry Henry,
While Villa organised their defences, surely conscious of the very real threat,
Henry spoke to the ref Mike, Halsey, and before the wall was set.

The ball stroked home through a mass of bodies, would his initiative be allowed?
Yes, the goal was good, despite the protests of the Villa players and crowd,
Villa felt Halsey had not indicated his permission for Henry to take the kick,
The travelling fans were laughing up until half time, while the Holt End were extremely sick.

Arsenal legend O'Leary's half-time team talk would not have been hard,
His new team behind 'unfairly' he felt, to the team for which he had starred,
Villa, fuelled by their anger and sense that justice had not been served,
Began the second half strongly, aiming to restore the parity they felt deserved.

Lucky for us their final pass and finishing could not match their desire,
Allback and Angel were not sparking while Kanu and Henry were on fire,
The home team strikers just simply could not catch a break,
It was the Nigerian's mesmerising quick feet once more that induced a mistake.

Kanu danced into the area leaving defenders flailing before hitting the deck,
Finally, and illegally, halted by a desperate Olaf Mellberg body check.
Henry stepped up hoping to increase O'Leary's and Villa's pain,
Was it ever in doubt, as he smashed home his 15th league goal of the campaign?

On 53 minutes, the match was in the bag and over as a contest,
The home team battled on valiantly but had met the Gunners at their best,
The news of United losing at Wolves had been warmly greeted,
Add 3 more points safely in the bag and another unbeaten month completed.

Not losing matches as Wenger had predicted was becoming a knack,
And with Cup matches left in January, his team led the Premier League pack,

REYES
9

While Wenger's lack of summer transfer activity still seemed a trifle odd,
He saw the January window as the time to spice up his league-leading squad.

Would a surprise swoop for a young Spanish striker prove again that 'Arsene knows'?
Jose Antonio Reyes arrived to keep our attacking players on their toes.
We hoped our young signing from Sevilla would quickly get into his stride,
An exciting new option, who could play through the middle as well as out wide.

P22 - WWWWDDWWWDWWWDDWDWWDWW

February

1st February Man City (H)

After two cup matches against Boro and the transfer window closed,
Back to the Premiership, unbeaten yes, but far from unopposed,
Spring in the air, the full focus on City, but where did we stand?
Only a point off our visitor's neighbours, United, but with a game in hand.

Vieira was injured, but his pleasurable pre-match duty, was a noble cause,
To welcome home, recently retired David Seaman, to rapturous applause,

The Romford Pele in for Paddy and still so trusted, he skippered the team,
Parlour, a ready, willing and able deputy, was every coach's dream.

From the off, the slick approach play was there, only the finishes were lacking,
The confidence of the Highbury faithful assured the team that they still had our backing,
Our early play was enterprising of which we failed to make the most,
Not sure which hurt Henry more, doing the splits as he shot or hitting the post.

Even Bobby P, scoring for fun of late, missed a gilt-edged chance,
It was from a perfectly weighted Henry ball, so nearly made in France,
Would the fans have to be satisfied with continually booing our old boy Nic?
Anelka may have starred for us once but the way he left, assured him stick.

Le Sulk was dispossessed, we broke with speed, and our old boy could only scowl,
Our counterattack resulted in a goal, and Nic was still screaming "foul!"
Parlour to Henry whose cross was deflected by Tarmat past David James,
One-Nil to the Arsenal we sang, happy the ref had ignored Anelka's claims.

The heavens opened that day, and the weather was becoming the boss,
Lehmann took no chances and punched away a dangerous swirling Sun Jihai cross,
Mad Jens was magnificent, saving a powerful Sylvain Distin header which,
Gathered pace as it bounced up awkwardly off the rain-slicked pitch.

O2

In such trying conditions it was a day both teams on their keepers depended,
Two top exponents of their craft, David and Jens both to be commended,
On 62 minutes, the moment for which the Highbury crowd had patiently waited,
The Arsenal debut of new striker Jose Antonio had been much anticipated.

Within minutes Reyes was denied by that man James a goal on his debut,
But it was now Arsenal pressure mounting, the home team turning the screw,
Yet still the City keeper heroically kept the red and white machine at bay,
Ljungberg limping off, a stunning save from Pires, was this still to be our day?

One man still believed, he always did, and whilst tension in the stadium grew,
That man, our talisman, unleashed a right-footed rocket, his aim unerringly true,
Merci Thierry, and bad luck James, the home support happy and calmer,
Though, with 7 minutes left on the clock, time for some more late drama.

Pantomime villain, once our Super Nic, on 90 minutes, pulled one back for City,
He went to get the ball from our net, Cole and Lehmann, the prevention committee,
So, Anelka, in a moment of madness, raised his hands to Ashley's face,
A red card was the obvious outcome, and we waved goodbye to our former ace,

A perfect end, to a soaking wet afternoon, and Wenger boys were two points clear,
After a hard-fought match, it had been our day, but was it to be our year?

7th February Wolves (A)

Wolves still struggling but battling had moved off the foot of the table,
Recently helping us, their defeat of United proved that they were able,
Compensating in passion and fight what they may have lacked in skill and finesse,
The Arsenal though were ready for the Black Country hustle and press.

Perhaps ready for the scrap, paying Wolves the renewed respect they were due,
Ljungberg was out so Wenger went for the extra midfielder in Edu,
The Brazilian swiftly repaying selection with a wonderful ball releasing Cole,
His pass into the box finding Bergkamp to half volley the opening goal.

Earlier in the season this might have led to a Wolves capitulation,
But Dave Jones' team were improving much to our frustration,
Toure and Campbell were kept busy and had to be on their toes,
In Dennis Irwin and new signing Carl Cort, our hosts had two wily old pros.

The veteran Irishman nearly drew his team level with a free kick past the post,
But then sloppy defending from a corner from which Wolves made the most,
Headed back for Romanian striker Ganea to volley home and give his side parity,
Cort nearly put his new side ahead at the break, Arsene's team talk given clarity.

2
23

Whatever the great man said to his team, it certainly worked a treat,
This second half Arsenal were marching to an entirely different beat,
The passing was quicker, with captain Vieira the tempo setter,
More movement, more confidence, in short more assured, everything was better.

The midfield combined to feed Pires, a stunning pass through the defensive line.
Henry on it in a flash, to dink over Paul Jones for Premier League number 99.
Reyes was on again for Dennis, the young Spaniard obviously trusted by Le Prof.
Wonderful to have a new talent who could add impetus right from the off.

However, it was existing French heroes who conjured Arsenal's third,
Pires a curling cross, for Paddy to volley back across the box, the sheer skill absurd,
At full stretch somehow managing to cut the ball back with accurate direction,
Toure not having to move to head home, with a goal of simple perfection.

One match closer to Arsene's dream, and another team put to the sword,
24 league matches unbeaten from the start of the season, a new club record,
Still two points ahead of Fergie's serial winners and in other news,
Now six points clear of the Russian oil rich wannabe West London Blues.

10th February Southampton (H)

A quick three-day turn around and a squad carrying injuries to revive,
Before the Saints coming marching into Islington, N5,
Parlour in for Super Fred and a full debut for Reyes in for the Ice Man,
Arsene had been easing our new signing in gradually, but time sped up the plan.

Jose was a very different player to Dennis, of course; more like Thierry in truth,
But our Dutch legend was no spring chicken and the Spaniard had zest and youth,
The travelling fans were not happy, and their discontent was clearly on show,
A return for Hoddle as manager was rumoured but the supporters, they said no!

Strachan had announced he would be stepping down, but was still popular for good reason,
Arsenal fans will recall he had taken them to Wembley the previous season,
The passion on the terraces seemed to inspire the south coast side,
The early exchanges were even, both teams early into their stride.

Pires who had five in six v the Saints had two efforts saved by Niemi early on,
Saints asked for a penalty, but the ref thought Ormerod, perhaps a diving swan,
We all appreciated Lauren for heading a Le Saux corner off the line,
Then a trademark Arsenal break with pace and incisiveness so divine.

Gilberto winning the ball back in our own half, as he did week in week out,
The Brazilian swiftly to Pires, and the next pass was never in doubt,
Henry knew his peer would find him, already travelling at full speed,
He beat the fullback, then from a tight angle, gave his team the lead.

Niemi got a hand to the shot but could not prevent Henry's ton,
It was his 100th in the English top-flight, we rose to salute as one,
The second half was equally even and twice Arsenal nearly came a cropper,
Both Ormerod and Baird brought super saves from our German shot-stopper.

Reyes was close to his first Arsenal goal, within inches of a Henry cross,
Perhaps sensing his team s tired legs, Clichy was sent on for Jose, by the boss,
Wee Gordan, sensing Arsenal's weariness, sent on two new strikers in the final ten,
He probably would have used Beattie and Pahars earlier if he had his time again.

The attacking intent was too little too late for Southampton though,
And the final flourish came from Arsenal and was a bit of a one man show,
Thierry s own ball-juggling skills and vision created a chance to seal the win,
Having beaten everyone, and Niemi, we were all stunned the ball did not go in.

Minutes later in injury time when Gilberto missed a ball Pires expertly cut back,
Henry was waiting to pounce and smash in his second in our final attack,

The Saints had matched and stretched us, but when all was said and done,
History will only remember them as invited guests to Henry's Room 101!

21st February Chelsea (A)

A week away from the Premier League seeking a third successive year of FA Cup glory,
As suggested at outset, however, this is only a league campaign story,
Only mentioning it now because our opponents in the cup were the same,
And to not do so by omission just this once would be a shame.

Why? Because Arsene rested Henry and played Reyes in his place,
And the baby-faced Spanish hitman only went and scored a brace,
Despite his heroics in the FA Cup win, Reyes would have to bide his time,
Dennis and Thierry reunited, glorious and proven partners in crime.

Edu favoured over the Romford Pele and Clichy back in the defence,
This was a huge match between title rivals, away support was tense,
With good cause it transpired, Arsenal sluggish from the off, to be blunt,
And inside a minute from kick off Gudjohnsen put a buoyant Chelsea in front.

And here is a phrase we seldom, if ever, had to say,
The goal came from Patrick Vieira giving the ball cheaply away,
The hosts were certainly keen to show their justified claims to the throne,
But they now had to contend with an angry Arsenal skipper keen to atone.

He won the ball in the centre circle and found Bergkamp in space,
Then set off up the pitch with his deceptive long-legged pace,
A sumptuous through ball from Dennis with the outside of his boot,
Found his captain, who did not even have to break stride to shoot.

So often a goal scorer from midfield for Arsenal in the past,
Astonishingly it was Vieira's first of the season, doubtful it would be his last,
And only a few minutes later, the Arsenal turnaround was completed,
As if we did not know by now it was a team that refused to be defeated.

Gilberto whipped an inswinger from the left that deceived Sullivan in mid flight,
The defenders failed to clear the danger and did not get a second bite,
Edu on the other hand watched the ball land, our number 17 stayed alert,
He slammed it home and peeled away kissing the gun on his shirt.

O2
4

The popular Brazilian deputy never let us down, a wonderful midfield technician,
His second goal of the campaign, both against this threatening opposition,
Chelsea were shell shocked for sure, but they did not take it lying down,
Lehmann liked to fool around, but that day he was far from a clown.

Saves from unlikely sources, Bridge and Terry kept the lead intact,
We expected a home team barrage in the second half and that proved to be a fact,
Mutu up front came alive and was a threat, suddenly playing with new verve,
But Toure and Campbell were magnificent and young Clichy held his nerve.

There were clearances, blocks, near misses survived that pivotal afternoon,
And our cause was helped by the Chelsea scorer, from hero to hapless loon,
Booked in the first half for a blatant dive, his second yellow for an obvious trip,
Without Gudjohnsen and Chelsea down to ten, Arsenal soon regained their grip.

Gilberto, who the Icelander had fouled, was twice denied an Arsenal third,
The home crowd left in droves before the end, only we Gooners could be heard,
It was difficult not to see this as a significant moment in the title race,
Chelsea vanquished, now nine behind us, and not able to live with our pace.

United too were faltering and a gap was beginning to appear,
With 12 matches left to play, Arsene's Gunners were seven points clear.

28th February Charlton (H)

Having dropped points at the Valley, Arsenal began determined to redress,
Starting the match at breakneck speed, like a runaway express,
Within two minutes a gorgeous 20-pass move handed a goal to Pires on a plate,
The Charlton players who could not get near the ball, had to just watch us create.

It was a landmark goal for Robert, his 50th for the Gunners,
This one a simple tap-in but who can forget all his stunners,
A few minutes later Bergkamp released Vieira who rampaged down the wing,
Unleashing a perfect low cross, instantly controlled and finished by the King.

Charlton were reeling, and must have wondered how they were still in the game,
Over-elaboration and Arsenal's long-range shooting were perhaps to blame,
The Addicks came out after the break beginning to believe,
Intent on making the most of what had seemed an unlikely reprieve.

In the first period Vieira and Edu had it all their own way,
After the break, Holland and Jensen were increasingly given a platform to play,
The players seemed to feel the game was won, and the comeback chances slim,
Arsene looked frustrated and the fans could empathise with him,

Then a soft foul on their main man, Di Canio, our players protesting in vain,
A quick free-kick in off the post, from Jensen, the tricky Dane,
So, at the end of an arduous month, it was all about protecting the lead,
Shoring up with Gilberto and Cygan, refusing to concede.

A match that started quickly, accelerated, and promised a cricket score,
That began like a celebratory party, but ended like an irksome chore,
February had passed with a quota of 15 points is what the records will show,
A month that ended with Arsenal nine points clear, after five wins in a row!

It seemed that we now had Chelsea and United punch drunk and on the ropes,
While in N5, was it now becoming expectations instead of hopes?

P27 WWWWDDWWWDWWWDDWDWWDWWWWWWW

March

March 13th- Blackburn (A)

Back after a two-week league break and a FA Cup quarter-final win,
Pompey the unlucky team to ship five and young Reyes got another 90 minutes in,
His ability to play either attacking role had persuaded the club to invest,
Jose offered options to an overplayed squad and, so far, he had impressed.

Dennis and Freddie were carrying minor knocks, so missed out at Ewood Park,
Gilberto was back though, and Reyes had recently offered an extra spark,
Ex-nemesis Andy Cole caused Lehmann to make a solitary first-half save,
But it truly was all Arsenal, a constant threat, attacking wave upon wave.

Friedal was again up to his goal-line heroics to prevent his side conceding,
With extra help from the referee, in this task he was succeeding,
On 26 minutes a cheeky steal by Henry, just after the ball left Friedal's hands,
Then calmly rolled into the empty net, wild away celebrations in the stands.

To spare their keeper's blushes, the Blackburn defenders the ref surrounded,
The goal was wrongly disallowed, we all knew their complaints unfounded,
The Arsenal players felt aggrieved and worked to put things to rights,
The sense of injustice burned and spurred the team on to new heights.

Jose and Bobby both went close, but Rovers held on to their clean sheet,
Surely, after the break though, they would regret labelling Henry a cheat,
Early in the second half Henry was tripped by Rovers' veteran Short,
Again, the home players hounded the ref, but it was obvious that Thierry was caught.

Despite being 25 yards out and facing a well-organised wall,
There was a certain inevitability about Arsenal's number 14 adding to his season's haul,
Yes, there was, a sublime up and over left poor Brad clutching air,
Faced with angry greatness, the American never had a prayer.

Despite their domination, the Gunners were only dangerously one ahead,
So the league leaders continued to seek a second to put the game to bed,
As so often was the case, it was Henry's compatriot, who shared the scoring strain,
Pires finishing a move he started himself, into double figures for the campaign.

20th March Bolton (H)

High winds at Highbury caused a 15-minute safety delay,
Which is not a phrase you will hear every day,
Still no love lost between the two rivals' coaches,
Both successful in their own way, with vastly different approaches.

Wenger's way was to pass through the opposition swiftly and slickly,
Big Sam's to get the ball in the box to Kevin Davies directly and quickly,
90 minutes to discover the style that succeeds,
Arsenal a win away from equalling a record shared by Liverpool and Leeds.

With records to equal, and clear in the Premier League race,
The Gunners straight out of the traps, playing with great early pace,
Vieira fed Henry who gave the Bolton defenders no time to think,
He had unleashed a rocket that hit the crossbar before they could blink.

Henry sees things that no one else does, the commentator's observation,
For a striker without equal, it was a perfect summation,
Still drooling about Thierry, while Edu and Bergkamp combined,
One French superstar on fire but there was another not far behind.

The Iceman with a delicate touch back for Pires who did the rest,
One touch, one look, and the ball, into the far corner caressed,
A well-oiled attacking force operating with complete coherence,
Henry was sure he had made it two, then a wonderful goal-line clearance.

The inevitable delayed only by a few minutes, and no more,
This time Thierry the assistor with a cross for his partner to score,
Seemingly, the home team in cruise control and threatening to run riot,
Keen anticipation from Gooners, the Bolton travelling fans were quiet.

But the visitors dangerous from set pieces, Sol and co had to stay awake,
Sadly, they failed to clear a corner, and Campo pulled one back before the break,
After the interval, Davies headed wide when he should have converted,
Henry shot a vicious volley that Jaaskelainen at full stretch, diverted.

Bolton frustrated our constant attacking endeavours, truth be told,
But equally they seldom looked capable of breaking the red and white stranglehold,
Pires drove over and Bergkamp drilled wide as the match fizzled out,
A massive cheer for a returning Freddie, the result never in doubt.

We would need the Super Swede fit and well for the season's home straight,
Starting with the following week, a heavyweight contest, no debate,
United were coming to town, and would fight clean or more likely dirty,
To prevent their rivals creating history and making it 30!

March 28th Manchester United (H)

Once again, for the fiercest of rivals, the battle was resuming,
For the media that week, the coverage understandably all consuming,
Tit for tat for seasons, but it looked like a North London power shift,
As Fergie's pre-season favourites arrived at Highbury 12 points adrift.

The animosity and ill feeling generated from September's angry stalemate,
Ensured it was a fixture, for which the footballing world could hardly wait,
The FA Cup draw had determined the giants would also play the following week,
First of all, though, the Arsenal focus was on maintaining the unbeaten streak.

Indeed, whatever one's allegiance, opinions, or pre-match views,
It was a game that United needed to win, and for Arsenal, just to not lose,
This was never a fixture for the inexperienced or faint-hearted,
Perhaps then a surprise that there was no Bergkamp, and Reyes started.

An injury for Gilberto, so Edu in with Paddy, Freddie back on the right,
Clichy in for Cole, which might have given us a bit of a fright,
Happily, no Beckham or Ronaldo on the right to give our youngster hell,
But then we saw Giggs starting there for young Gael to try and repel.

To be fair to United, they needed the win and they set the tone,
They were desperate, by any means, to stop Arsenal taking their throne,
Arsenal were keen to show they were worthy of the Premiership crown,
Scholes should have scored before Freddie was denied by a blocking Wes Brown.

The Swede was then kept out by Roy Carrol with Reyes well positioned square,
With his eyes firmly set on a goal, sadly Ljungberg did not see him there,
Lehmann scrambled well to his right keeping out a volley from Djemba Djemba,
Tackles were flying in all over the pitch, it seemed a continuation of September.

No surprise then to see Paddy booked for a challenge on his nemesis Ruud,
Our skipper protested of course but the foul was rather crude,
The tension in the stands increased, as in the tackles flew,
It was not long before, on the touchline, that Arsene and Alex were at it too.

A frenetic half ended with Neville and Henry having penalty claims denied,
United's skipper Keane almost had the last word, but his shot flashed wide,
The pressure was clearly on United as the second half got underway,
Already 12 points behind Arsenal with eight matches after this to play.

It got worse for Fergie, who could only watch on with disbelief,
As a 30-yard bullet was fired by Arsenal's Commander in Chief,
A convincing No. 1, perhaps one would argue that Roy Carroll was not,
But even a world-class keeper would not have got near Henry's thunderbolt shot.

It was all on United to find a way back, as all defending champions would,
But to beat us from one-nil down in the league, when no one else could?
Only three minutes later, Sol clumsy on Giggs, but penalty appeals waved away,
Undeniable relief, as it might have been given on another day.

The obvious implication that the Welsh winger had dived angered United,
Was this to be the touch paper on a comeback ignited?
Without the experience and know-how of Ashley would Arsenal's backline crack?
As the visitors threw everything at us in attack after attack.

Fergie really went for it throwing on Saha and Solskjaer up top,
Leaving Arsenal with three in-form international strikers to stop,
On 86 minutes the super subs combined to level the score,
We all knew then that we had a grandstand finish in store.

Both main strikers had headers to win it, close but no cigar,
Lehmann saved from Van Nistlerooy and Henry headed over the bar,
Honours even on the afternoon and another top-flight record earned,
Perhaps it was the day United lost hope, where the title was concerned.

A dozen points behind us, with only eight to play, was too much for the Red Devils,
A match for us on the day, but over the season Arsenal were at different levels,
Seven points clear of Chelsea in second, so unless our form fell off the cliff,
As April beckoned new champions, it was a case of when and not if!

For the media it was a now a case of remembering Arsene's outrageous claim,
That his team was capable of going a league season without losing a single game.

P30 WWWWDDWWWDWWWDDWDWWDWWWWWWWWWD

April

April 9th Liverpool (H)

This is a Premiership story, which was made clear at the beginning,
As a result, it has been a joyous tale, largely about Arsenal winning,
And whilst on Europe and the FA Cup we will not overly dwell,
For context, the reader needs to know it had been the week from hell.

Without Henry dumped out of the FA Cup semi-final by Paul Scholes,
Then ousted from the Champion's League by Chelsea on away goals,
After so much disappointment and a sense of deflation,
The visit of a resurgent Liverpool was a stern examination.

Did we still believe his team could chase the undefeated league season grail?
Certainly, the media vultures were hovering, hoping we would fail,
Henry had missed the FA Cup semi but was back in the side,
It was landmark day, one that in hindsight should fill us all with pride.

30 hurdles overcome and his team so far ahead of the pack,
And Wenger has achieved this, with always one arm tied behind his back,

It was match 31, and finally Arsene was in manager's seventh heaven,
It was the first match of the campaign where he could pick his first 11.

Mad Jens, joined by Lauren, Kolo, Big Sol, and Cole,
Freddie, Bobby, Gilberto, Paddy, and Dennis in the hole,
With the Thierry up top, the star who just continued to shine,
Finally on this incredible Premier League campaign, all our stars align.

The Highbury crowd were nervous, after such an awful week, of course,
Hoping that their team would climb immediately back on the horse,
Mild anxiety at outset was soon to become genuine worry,
One-nil down after five minutes, Hypia and Liverpool in a hurry.

There seemed little doubt that Arsenal's hangover was real,
We were hanging on as Gerrard prompted his team with such zeal,
Largely on the back foot and with confidence seemingly low,
Our passing usually so swift and purposeful was wayward and slow.

The first 30 minutes from the Gunners was weak and error strewn,
Liverpool were creating chances at will, it could be a long afternoon,

The commentator asked, obviously believing we had run out of steam,
Is this the beginning of the end of Arsenal's title dream?

The answer was an emphatic no, as Gilberto won the ball back (his hobby!),
Then, as he often did, passed it simply and swiftly to Bobby,
As it had been so frequently, it was the Pires and Henry show,
The brilliant winger fed the lethal striker, already in full flow.

Henry found the far corner, the perfect precision after just one glance,
Like so many keepers before and since, Dudek had no chance,
Perhaps the equaliser would settle the nerves of the boys in red and white,
Could they see it through to half time, sadly no not quite.

Gerrard magnificently fed Michael Owen and he made no mistake,
Arsenal trailed by that goal, so now up to Arsene's chat in the half-time break.
Would the champions elect pass this true test of character and bottle?
It was an unequivocal yes, as Arsenal began the half at full throttle.

Freddie with a precise first-time pass found Bobby running through,
A prodded finish from Pires and the belief was felt anew,
The crowd were still singing Super Rob when we struck again a minute later,
It was a goal to live long in the memory, you will not see too many greater.

Was he the greatest striker in the world, on that day who could quibble,
Henry was barely in the opposition half when he began his mazy dribble,
He side-stepped one, Diddy Hamann, then left Carragher on the grass,
Biscan was next to look a fool, as Thierry balletically glided past.

The precision finish at the end of a run that had left chaos trailing in its wake,
2-1 up to 3-2 down in 2 mesmerising minutes, tough for the Scousers to take,
Houllier introduced a fresh striker Baros, endeavouring to regain parity,
But this was now an Arsenal fully focused, playing with a renewed clarity.

Edu on for an exhausted Pires, who left to well-earned and warm applause,
The Highbury fans saw an exhausted hero who had given all for our cause,
We then got want we all wanted, a hattrick for our hero number 14,
An outrageous assist from Bergkamp, a pass others would not have tried or seen.

At the end of a week when the media had called Arsene's team out,
The team rallied for him, when those outside the club showed such doubt,
After a week that saw the naysayers predict that his team might be spent,
His first team stood up proud with a true statement of their intent.

April 11th Newcastle (A)

Arsenal could now focus on the league, that well-worn phrase!
It was true, but this was a second match in three days,
After three matches in six days, would the fourth be arriving too soon?
It was never any easier trip to the Northeast to face the Toon.

After the heavy schedule, certain exhausted players needed to be rested,
Once again, all eyes on Arsenal, their squad depth to be tested,
Freddie was out, and Pires and Bergkamp dropped to the bench,
In came a Brazilian, a Spaniard and the surprise was someone French.

Edu and Reyes had been playing, but the start for Wiltord unexpected,
It was December, the last time Sylvain had been selected,
Bobby Robson had guided the Magpies to fifth in the league,
His team hoping to take advantage of the visitors' fatigue.

The home team began brightly, were Kolo and Sol ready for Shearer?
As it happened the threat from Bellamy soon became clearer,
Lehmann twice denied the lively Welsh striker, the second save top draw,
The forward convinced he had scored, watched the one-handed save with awe.

Arsenal looked mentally jaded, their heavy schedule to blame,
But early storm weathered, Henry dragged his team into the game,
Prevented from scoring by a last-ditch Aaron Hughes block you had to applaud,
Then a curling shot a whisker wide when we thought he had scored.

Reyes not wanting to be outdone was also in full flow,
A wonderfully deft chip over Woodgate, his talents now on show,
Edu arrived right on time, Jose's lovely cross to greet,
Another amazing block, this time by Bernard, maintained the Toon's clean sheet.

A dodgy back pass then put Wiltord in, his right foot once so trusty,
Scuffed the chance, with Given stranded, Sylvain's touch was rusty,
The second half followed a familiar pattern, the home team starting well,
The Gallowgate obviously roaring their boys on, victory they could smell.

Was this game too far Arsene's boys, the away fans certainly fretting,
More so, when Bernard impressing at both ends, fired into the side netting,
The travelling fans then found their voice and out came the obvious song,
You thought that you had scored, you were wrong, you were wrong.

Again, the resilience of these incredible players, there for all to witness,
Conserving energy and playing on the counter, with such will and such fitness,
It was an afternoon when the character of the squad clearly came across,
Closing in on the title yes, but more, they would not accept a loss,

We went close to winning all three points, the margins often so slight,
Henry rounded Given, only to see his effort come off the upright.

One last chance to win the match, a leaping Toure set to be the hero,
Saw his glancing header land in Given's arms, we settled for zero-zero,
In the context of the mental and physical strain of four matches in eight days,
A hard-fought draw at St James Park was deserving of high praise.

16th April Leeds United (H)

Arsenal were closing in on the title, they had done the hard yards,
How much had changed in a year, one never felt losing to Leeds on the cards,
Not the disruptors of 2003, having sacked Peter Reid and turned to Eddie Gray,
Now more a question about if they could extend their Premier League stay.

Wiltord kept his place wide, and Vieira back with Silva in midfield,
Clichy in for Cole and Pires back, with Ljungberg as yet not fully healed,

O2
14

The magnificent duo reunited to worry a highly porous Leeds defence,
Henry keen to edge ahead in the Golden Boot race, at Shearer's expense.

As it transpired it was a day for Thierry to make merry,
Assisted by Gilberto but also Leeds defender Michael Duberry,
Within six minutes, Bergkamp, ever the creator, put Pires through,
Bobby smashed the ball home, with a gallic merci beaucoup.

The winger didn't have to break stride, a perfect weight of pass,
The mercurial French master benefiting from the Dutch artist's class,
Leeds toiled and blustered but defensively were far from compact,
It was only a matter of time before Henry got in on the act.

Gilberto, a perfect defence splitting pass, poor Duberry, the hapless chap,
He had endeavoured on his own, to spring an offside trap,
Henry was on it like a flash, and rounded Robinson with ease,
It was 3-0 minutes later, and the visitors were on their knees.

A Bergkamp and Wiltord neat one-two into the box had worked like a charm,
Dennis was setting to finish the move, when denied by Duberry's arm,
Henry stood over the spot and calmly waited for Robinson to commit,
Then chipped it down the middle, confidence in the extreme, you had to admit.

With barely half an hour played, Leeds were in need of Arsenal's pity,
Vieira flashed a header wide before the break, but his team were sitting pretty,

Happily, for the home support, the second half continued in the same vein,
It was one of the most impressive days, of a seriously impressive campaign,
Number four, a repeat of number two, as Gilberto again released our attacking ace,
The Brazilian's through ball again well timed, but made perfect by Henry's pace.

Was a hattrick enough for Arsenal's number 14 under the floodlights so bright?
No was the answer, he secured his first four-goal haul on that crazy night,
A solo effort of sumptuous brilliance, as he ran 35 yards like a gazelle,
Even as the desperate Leeds defenders tried to trip him, he finished it so well.

The Sky pundit that evening, Andy Gray, was not even going out on a limb,
In stating I have been in football 25 years and never seen anything like him!
In the last 20 Arsene was able to give three stars a well-earned rest,
Pires, Bergkamp, and Gilberto had all been at their best.

More minutes for Reyes and Edu, and great to see the Romford Pele fit,
Ray was one of our own and we all wanted him back to do his bit,
Jose Antonio should have made it six with seconds left to play,
He could not break his league duck, but we knew he would soon have his say.

25th April Tottenham (A)

United could not catch us after losing to Liverpool the day before,
Then Newcastle beat Chelsea, we could not have asked for more,
The stage was set, as it had been 33 years earlier, for history to be made again,
The Arsenal set to make the short trip to win the league at White Hart Lane.

The anticipation levels through the roof, to secure the title at our enemy's joint,
Spurs desperate to win, and Arsenal Champions elect, only needing a point,
Our not-so-noisy neighbours were fighting for pride, oh and to avoid relegation,
The Gunners again to prove, beyond doubt, they were the finest in the nation.

Sentimentality perhaps from Arsene when it came to his selection,
A nod to an incredible servant to our club, and one high in Wenger's affection,
So much Arsenal glory for Parlour, 13 wonderful years had passed,
He earned the right to start this NLD, we sensed it would be his last.

In 1971, we had to wait 88 minutes for Kennedy to win it at their place,
With the momentum of 33 unbeaten, we felt in 2004, this would not be the case,
The well-founded confidence took only minutes to translate on the field,
A goal to the good three minutes in and we all believed the title sealed.

Henry collected inside his own box and set off with ball at feet,
Released to Dennis on the left, his pass inside the fullback was so sweet,
The Iceman looked up to see who had kept up with the rapid pitch-long break,
It would need a super man with a massive stride for the ground to make.

And there his skipper was to meet the cross, his right leg outstretched ,
If this were not Thierry, Dennis and Paddy, it might be a story so far-fetched,
These were not sporting mortals; these were players who defied all odds,
To those of us blessed to witness their exploits, these were footballing gods.

Keane worked tirelessly for Spurs, and in truth Lehmann made a save or two,
But it was Spurs, so we all knew who would step up next from our heavenly crew,
Scoring against the Middlesex mob was, after all, a certain Frenchman's hobby,
In this instance it was Dennis and Paddy combining to set up Super Bobby.

Pires had begun the move, that he finished, and it was another stunner,
His sicth against the local rivals, in only his fourth season, a Gunner,
The home side seemed to be fighting against a tidal wave of red and white,
In fairness, they came out for the second half with far more fight.

BARC
CH

It had taken a woeful first-half display from his team for Pleat to decide,
That this was a North London derby, it was imperative to restore some pride,
Defoe, joined Keane and Kanute, which signalled intent and a new aggression,
Would this three-pronged attack make a better impression?

It was Defoe who fed Michael Brown who slid the ball to Redknapp,
And to be fair to Jamie, his unerring, swerving shot found a gap,
It was more of a contest for sure, both teams going blow for blow,
But this was never the day for them to step out from under our shadow.

Then in injury time as victory seemed it was ours to claim,
A moment of rashness as Mad Jens lived up to his nickname,
The German was penalised for a foul on Keane as a Brown corner came in,
To be fair he had climbed on the striker, so we had to take it on the chin.

Keane slammed home the penalty and the points were therefore shared,
But as the final whistle blew, ultimately none of us cared,
82 points, 34 unbeaten matches, and champions again with four matches to play,
In the grand scheme of things, two dropped points forgotten, as this was our day.

To celebrate as Premier League Champions on Tottenham's pitch was simply bliss,
The footballing gods aligned that Sunday, as it did not get better than this,

To watch our players, particularly Sol, dance on the White Hart Lane grass,
Knowing we won it Wenger's way, with belief in his style and always with class.
Winning football could indeed be art, and that Arsene had undoubtedly showed,
And we held that thought as we danced back down the Seven Sisters Road.

P34 WWWWDDWWWDWWWDDWDWWDWWWWWWWWWDWDWW

May

May 1st Birmingham (H)

And now suddenly unique football history was more than achievable,
Four more games to do in the league, what all felt inconceivable,
To go a league campaign unbeaten was a feat few could comprehend,
And in the 21st century it's 38 matches, with respect to Preston North End.

As you might imagine the atmosphere in the build-up was festive and hearty,
Freddie and Jose were back for the May Day Highbury party,
In fairness, there was an element of after the Lord Mayor's show,
And the party on the pitch, at least, never truly got into full flow.

With a job well done, a slight loss of edge from the players was hardly confusing,
We were all still celebrating, and now it was certainly about NOT losing,
The first half was tepid, the Blues, well organised and resolute,
Arsenal controlled possession but in the final third failed to execute.

A Reyes volley wide from a Bergkamp cross the closest we came,
Even Henry, the newly crowned PFA Player of the Year, was easy to tame,
Perhaps reminded by Arsene, that a party was better with entertainment,
The players upped their game to overcome Birmingham's containment.

Again, innovative Thierry thinking to which Blues neighbours Villa testified,
Another trademark quickly taken freekick, wall and keeper beaten, inches wide,
Sadly, it was an ex-Tottenham player who elicited the match's first save of note,
Thankfully, Clemence's effort was straight down Jens' throat.

Arsene made positive subs, with Pires and young Jeremie entering the fray,
A rest for Robert Pires and still no elusive first league goal for Jose,
As the famous clock's hands moved on, it was to be the rarest of games,
Only the second Highbury stalemate, despite strong late Bergkamp penalty claims.

The crowd were still basking in Premier League glory, but Arsene gave them a lift,
A 90th-minute one to precise, and we all understood his gift,

On came our veteran hero Keown for his seventh league appearance of the season,
And the educated home fans well knew Wenger's reason.
The games were running out for Martin and for a medal he needed ten,
With three matches remaining we knew we would see the old warhorse again!

4th May Portsmouth (A)

In the autumn Pompey appointed a Director of Football, it was the new way,
However, it was not for Harry Redknapp, who had been reluctant to stay,
He and Chairman Manderic had the most public of spats,
So, the new man, Velimir Zajec ended up wearing both hats.

The Croatian had steered his team to safety with three games still to play,
Arsenal hoped his players were mentally 'on the beach' to use an old cliche,
An eyebrow or two raised when Arsene gave David Bentley his first league start,
We knew he was a confident lad though, chomping at the bit to play his part.

Parlour back in with Paddy and Reyes selected over Bergkamp was not so odd,
But it was a shock to see no Bergkamp, Gilberto, Edu, and Pires even in the squad,
Why was Le Prof taking such a risk, seemingly taking his foot of the pedal?
Or looking at the bench that day, was he just ensuring loyal servants a medal?

Pompey's attack had our first choice backline troubled in uncharacteristic fashion,
The dual threat of Yakuba and Lua Lua played with pace and passion,
The first half saw the teams trading offensive blows with defences looking porous,
The home supporters sensed weakness, Play up Pompey was in full chorus.

The Romford Pele unleashed a magnificent curler, Hislop was equal to it,
Lehmann saved from The Yak, before Lua Lua was clean through and blew it,
On 28, we thought the moment had arrived for our young Spanish star,
Reyes released a rocket, which sadly skimmed off Sol and rebounded off the bar.

A long ball deflected off Kolo saw Yakubu leave Campbell in his wake,
Jens was out quickly but it was a tight-angled finish the striker was able to make,
An instant reaction by the Champions, the setup from Freddie simply divine,
Henry incredulous to see his bullet pushed onto the post and then bounce up off the line.

Thankfully, the second half began the way the first had ended,
Playing on the front foot, surely our unbeaten streak could be extended,
Within minutes, the moment we had anticipated for so long,
A partially cleared cross fell to Reyes, and his volley was strong.

This was his moment, and the travelling Gooners who were there,
We will long remember the Spaniard's celebratory jump high in the air,

For the early part of the second half, it was Pompey who were in trouble,
Were it not for a slip when he was in the clear, it was nearly a Jose double,

Bentley's debut was over on the hour, perhaps a substitution pre-agreed,
The experience of Kanu, to help retain possession, a useful trait indeed,
Then with 13 minutes to play, Yakuba clean through, the unbeaten run in danger,
Again to our rescue came Lehmann, our new keeper, a true game changer.

The German had a hot temper for sure but when needed was calm and chilled,
Many clean sheets, and match-turning saves, Seamen's gloves were filled,
Young Aliadiere came on for injury time, joined also by Martin K,
Jeremie needed one more for his gong, and Keown two, with only two to play.

It had been an anxious 90 minutes, in which fortunes had ebbed and flowed,
Once again the great man repaid loyalty, and faith in his squad he showed,
Arsene had trusted his young French striker on many occasions that season,
With 400+ Arsenal appearances, he was rewarding Keown with good reason.

The match will be remembered for the aftermath, not the game so much,
When the home crowd applauded Thierry off the pitch, such a lovely touch,
Educated fans who recognised greatness, though he starred for the opposition
Football lovers simply admiring the tricks of the league's number one magician.

May 9th Fulham (A)

For the home side, not truly at home, this was a celebratory bash,
It was a farewell to Loftus Road party but one that Arsenal hoped to crash,
Fulham under Chris Coleman, were in form, and had one simple mission,
To win their last home match, and consolidate a top ten position.

Not happy with two draws having secured the third title of his reign,
Arsene wanted to be winning, ahead of the final match champagne,
Parlour continued and Reyes retained his place after scoring,
It was hardly a surprise with the Spaniard's confidence soaring.

Arsenal started strongly with Parlour threading a ball through to Freddie,
Van der Saar, our nemesis at Highbury, again proved to be more than ready,
But then minutes later the Dutch maestro with a moment he'd wish to forget,
A horrible mis-control of a back pass presented a pressing Reyes an empty net.

The keeper had tried to side-step the Spaniard but got his feet in a muddle,
The Arsenal players jubilant in an unexpected early joyous huddle,
It seems as well that we had been presented with such an early gift,
As the unwanted post-title winning lethargy was proving hard to lift.

Former Gunner, Boa Morte shot straight at Jens, when put through one on one,
When he was our player we wished that he could shoot like he could run,
Another early Wenger buy, Moritz Volz was out to prove a point as well,
He certainly was impressing us that afternoon, had we been wrong to sell?

In truth, Lauren had made the number two slot his own, before Dicko had retired,
Converting him from midfield to right back, a move that was inspired,
It was Volz who set up Malbranque, after leading Cole a merry dance,
Thankfully, his shot curled past the post, the French striker spurning his chance.

Cole then lost the young German and went close with a headed attempt,
Henry was awfully quiet, it seemed even he was from the malaise not exempt,
The honest reflection of the second half from an Arsenal perspective,
Just holding on defensively and offensively entirely ineffective.

Hard to recall many instances where the boys in yellow and blue carried a threat,
While Fulham's increasing and justified confidence was making us sweat,

Volz drilled a low shot narrowly wide when he looked certain to score,
Coleman sent on two strikers, McBride and Collins John, looking for at least a draw.

With three attackers on the pitch, Arsenal's back four were being stretched,
Even on the visage of the ever-calm Wenger, worry lines were etched,
Our players looked to be devoid of energy of which the home team had plenty,
Clichy was introduced to add a fifth defensive player for the final 20.

Creating modern history over a long season, though, was always going to be tough,
After so much swagger and dominance, this was horribly nail-biting stuff,
But hang on we did until Fulham finally seemed to thankfully run out of steam,
The obligatory late introduction of Keown, he and we were still living the dream.

To do what most believe cannot believe or imagine is in Spanish incognoscible,
In other words, perhaps, making the deemed impossible, possible,
Arsene and his team stood on the threshold of achieving such a feat,
One last match at the Home of Football, one more match to avoid defeat.

May 15th Leicester (H)

When Arsene had said what he said, the football world quietly sniggered,
Everyone, even we Gooners, doubted, and nobody actually figured,

that with one match remaining, it would be well beyond cynicism and jokes,
The Cool Cat and his Magic Hat stood on the precipice of history, folks.

On this May Day, the footballing world were no longer poking fun,
Only Leicester stood between Arsene and what no one thought could be done,
Those of us lucky enough to have the 'Golden Ticket' were in early that day,
Yes, a party mood, expectancy, but nerves also that we could not downplay.

For only the second match of the season, Arsene could draw on perfection,
With all fit, the 11 who started would always have been his selection,
To think we were worried that Lehmann was our only major summer addition,
38th match in a row, and after losing Seaman, it was an easy transition.

Lauren, an unsung hero, so consistent in defence and in support of the attack,
Toure, we had forgotten our panic that he had never played centre back,
The tower of strength in Super Sol, who led by example and a clench of his fist,
Only a player of his stature could have ensured Big Tone had not been missed.

Ashley Cole was up and down the flank, his relationship with Bobby so strong,
Only 23, homegrown, and the best in Europe, we had known all along,
The quietly essential presence that was Gilberto, no finer footballing brain,
Spot danger, tackle, or intercept, pass and attacks launched again and again.

Our skipper Vieira, fighting in our midfield trenches since the triumphs of 98,
Best midfielder in the league, but boy as a leader he had stepped up to the plate,
No longer with red hair but still Arsenal through and through,
Freddie ran all day, week in and week out, chipping in a vital goal or two.

Few superlatives left for Robert Pires, phenomenal flair and skill,
14 goals, countless assists, and his presence made Henry better still,
Just off the front was the Ice Man, the older statesman of this team,
To have Bergkamp's vision and passing at ten, every front man's dream.

Thierry Henry had raised the bar, that even we felt impossible to raise,
With one more goal for 30, our 14 simply continued to thrill and amaze,
The anticipation was palpable, perhaps we believed we had done it already,
The celebrations so close to starting early, with a shot just wide from Freddie.

Then a stunning Henry freekick, an up and over corker,
Annoyingly well tipped over by Leicester's former Spurs keeper, Ian Walker.
To be denied the lead by an ex-Tottenham was a frustrating bore,
But moments later it was worse as an ex-Gunner popped up to score.

A Foxes break, and a Frank Sinclair cross which Jens had just not read,
Found its way back into our goal courtesy of Paul Dickov's head,

It would be fair to say Highbury was stunned, and momentary tension gripped,
Leicester were playing party poopers who were no following history's script.

On the pitch however, the players stayed cool and were not so easily phased,
Bobby P had a stinging drive well saved and the home crowd decibels were raised,
It was to be a long half-time interval, going in behind was a rarity,
Most of us still shocked and appalled Leicester's outrageous temerity!

Within a minute of the restart the boys were set to regain control,
Destiny back in our hands when Sinclair hauled down Ashley Cole,
The fullback found with the type of pass only Bergkamp could execute,
Clumsily bundled to the ground in the box, the penalty was not in dispute.

Henry calmly slotted home, further adding to his place in Arsenal folklore,
The first man since Ronnie Rook to score 30 in the league, 56 years before,
On 66 minutes, the place in English football's chronicles forever sealed,
By the finest centre midfielder in the league, our leader on the field.

Paddy began the move, a sideways pass to Dennis, and then began his run,
For the Iceman's pass with the inside of his boot to find him, probably 100-1,
A pass so outrageous and of such insane quality and fitting of the occasion,
Vieira's control and rounding of the keeper the second part of a glorious equation.

From then on, it was Arsenal all the way and no further Leicester devilry,
Would be allowed to spoil the full-on and much-deserved revelry,
Three more came who had contributed so much and thoroughly earned the right,
Edu, Reyes and of course Big Martin for his last outing in red and white.

Keown warranted his medal, he smiled and acknowledged our cheers.
His part at Old Trafford never forgotten, nor his service through the years.
Strange to think back to that September day now, how were we to know.
The Van Nistlerooy miss was the closest we had been to a loss, at six down with 32 still go!

The final whistle met with mixed emotions, joy, and certainly relief,
Ecstasy, camaraderie, exhaustion, and still pinch us for disbelief,
The celebrations on the pitch were long, time for us fans to show appreciation,
For our team, and our wonderful leader, who had ideas above his station.

The first foreign coach to win our league had done so again and refusing,
to accept, that the squad he had built, could not do so without losing.
He joined his players soaking up the adulation so richly merited.
No longer was this success built on a defence he had inherited.

This was his team, moulded to his principles and to his artistic style,
A team that combined beautiful Wenger football, with strength and guile,

Joined by his daughter Lea on the pitch, adorned with his medal, so proud!
He shared the moment with her, as she hurled plastic trophies into the crowd.

Perhaps the footballing world accepted now that his conviction was not conceit,
Whilst we just basked in the glory of our team and marvelled at their feat,
To go 38 matches in a gruelling league without one loss still seemed so crazy,
Many memories of that day in one sense but simultaneously a bit hazy.

Thierry and Sol sat chatting on the Highbury turf, their achievement sinking in,
Me, grinning inanely, deciding which pubs I would be drinking in.

Played 38

WWWWDDWWWDWWWDDWDWWDWWWWWWWWWDWDWWDDWW

LOST NONE!!!

EPILOGUE

Twenty years have passed and in leaner times we've had these memories to treasure,
To this day the success of Arsenal in 2003/4 is still the benchmark measure,
Others can conquer the league with more wins, more points, or even more goals,
It is not the same as winning without losing at all, they know it in their souls,
Even Arsene's arch-rival Fergie has graciously admitted this fact to be true,
Not bad for the bespectacled unknown, ignorantly labelled Arsene Who?

The Premier League powerbrokers knew Arsene and Arsenal had set a new high bar,
He had dreamed the impossible dream and reached the unreachable star,
They presented us with a different trophy, they have not made one like it since,
For each new pretender that comes along whose fans themselves try to convince,
We laugh at their presumption as they get a little cocky or far too bold,
And we respond with one simple question "Is yours GOLD?"

Perhaps Arsene and Arsenal will remain sole purveyors of what can't be done,
Perhaps one day another team will play 38 matches without losing a single one,
Until that day, should it ever arrive, we say bon merci Arsene, you did us proud,
From Double Double to Invincibubble, and STILL a cut above the envious crowd!

I would like to thank Arsene Wenger, Pat Rice, David Dein and a legendary group of players, without whom this book would not have been possible.

My gratitude also to Dave an Anu, for checking my words and rhymes!!